So you want to TEACH?

Michael Clark

BROWN
DOG
BOOKS

For,

My beautiful wife Lin, whose love and support have been
constant over the last 31 years (and a few broken mugs!).
My children, Stephen, Natalie, James and Ben who I still learn
from today. My mum, Maureen and late Dad Fred,
for their upbringing, love and support. For the in-laws, Val and
Ken, for all the babysitting duties during
teacher training and beyond.

Thank you all xx

Contents

Foreword

SO YOU WANT TO TEACH?

The following describes some of my own personal experiences during eighteen years of working in secondary and further education. I have altered the names of the establishments and pupils, but all incidents are true.

It is not intended to offer deep psychological theories into learning, or have descriptive passages like a gripping novel. No, it is only a short, light read that will give a glimpse into my world as a teacher.

I expect that every person who has taught, or who is teaching today, could give many such accounts.

You can agree or disagree with my thoughts, but above all, as with any activity, and most importantly, I hope you enjoy.

1 Introduction

What do you want to do when you grow up? That age-old question that you are asked as a child. Well, my answer was never, 'I want to be a teacher'.

My passion and my dream was to play football. Like many professional footballers' autobiographies that I have read, I enjoyed being down the park or in the school field adjacent to our council house. We used to enjoy the school field as the goals were left up 24/7. We squeezed through a damaged feather edge fence to get in and, when the old fence was replaced, we would scale the rusty front gates. With a church at the far end, we had roughly a two-thirds-sized pitch to hone our skills. The problem with the school field was that, after about twenty minutes, we would be evicted. An Irish fella, with a feathery grey mop of hair would pull up in his beige Ford Cortina Ghia and insist we vacate the pitch. Some of us used to protest and argue that we were doing no harm, but we always left. Evidently at some stage the church stained-glass windows had been broken, so 'Paddy' was always on hand to be the enforcer. I must stress, we did not break any windows as my brother, friends and I always played down the opposite end.

My football career made it to non-league level, or should I say semi-professional as it is known now? I do have a chuckle at this: semi-pro has a sense of grandeur. I got paid £5 per game when I made the first team, so it put some petrol in the tank. Crucially, though, I stopped enjoying football for a time and to become a professional you have to be selfish, single-minded and ruthless. As a 6' 5" lean centre half, at times I could be ruthless, but only if the centre forward wanted to put himself around. Otherwise I just wanted to play. Most managers wanted me to go through everyone and everything. I wanted to be a little more cultured.

Dad always told me, 'Make sure you work hard at school,' knowing that you should always have a backup plan. Even at a young age, I knew it wasn't nice to be selfish. Growing up with an older sister, brother and foster sister taught me it was good to share. Dad did spoil me with my football boots, though, and the smell of my first pair of Adidas World Cup 78 boots remains with me today.

My first career objective was to become a physiotherapist. Ideally it would be in sport, but I knew it would start in the NHS. After passing my 'O' levels, including English and Maths, I returned to sixth form to complete the 'A' levels required to become a physio. School didn't feel the same. The majority of our great football team were not there (we had won the London Cup the season before). In my first 'A' level Maths lesson I was greeted with: "Who are you and what are you doing here?"... "Maths I hope!" My teacher then proceeded to write on his overhead projector and I was clueless.

Mum noticed I was disillusioned. At the same time, Nan (my mum's mum) was in a coma after suffering a stroke. Some memories always stay with you. When Nan was well, and kissing her goodbye as we left, her face was always luxurious and soft, peach-like. It was a difficult time, but after a conversation with Mum, we established that I enjoyed woodwork. Dad was a self-employed carpenter / builder, so after a discussion with George, the governor at Surrey Joinery, a local firm, I started as a YTS trainee on £25 a week. This in turn led to my bench joinery apprenticeship. At the end of my apprenticeship, as well as learning a trade, I had achieved craft, advanced and supplementary levels in Carpentry and Joinery. With English and Maths already under my belt, it proved a good decision to take the advanced course, although I didn't know how important it would be until later in my career.

After four years in the joinery shop, supplying and sometimes fitting joinery work, I went self-employed as a carpenter and joiner subcontractor. Lin was expecting our first child, so I needed a better rate of pay to support us all. I had become a tradesman, which to this very day I am proud to say I still am. At this stage, teaching had not crossed my mind. That thought was still a few years away.

2 Where does teaching start?

Upbringing. This is where teaching starts. Traditionally it would be classed as having a mum and dad, in a happy, safe, family environment. Modern times have changed. Who is to say that the happy environment cannot be set by two mums or two dads, not forgetting those single parents who have to do the work of two?

I recently read a book whilst on holiday. The author described some people as ordinary and normal, comparing people to him, an adventure racer. As life is precious, each and every one of us is different. I would disagree and state that no one is ordinary. We all have different experiences and something special to give. Normal? What classifies as my normal could be vastly different from yours.

As a child we had boundaries, house rules to follow, rotas to complete, pets to look after, bedtime routines, bedtime stories to read or read to us. We had fun, played games with each other, at times fought and argued, but always looked after each other. Punishments if we were out of line. Dinner and teatimes would be together when possible, around a table, not in front of a TV, talking to each other, laughing, joking, debating. Occasionally on a tray in front of the TV to watch 'The Big Match'. So I grew up loving and respecting Mum and Dad.

Lin had similar experiences with her upbringing, so naturally with our own children we had the same process. Lin is a brilliant mum. Whilst training for my different job roles, Lin set our family routine. It gives a family structure, support, morals, love. This type of upbringing can be rejected of course, but if we end up with caring family members who can also think about others' feelings and needs, not just their own, then to me that is a good upbringing.

So learning starts with your first experiences, your early memories, the love and care afforded to you. Learning by example. Seeing your mum and dad work hard to provide for you, the standard of behaviour to be followed.

Upbringing. This is where teaching starts.

Woodwork

3 Why become a teacher?

Mum was a primary school teacher. She had completed her teacher training whilst I was at primary school. I spent many an afternoon after school being looked after by Sylvie, Mum's friend. Sylvie's daughter, Michelle, went to the same school, so I would go and play there and have tea whilst Mum was at college or school.

PRIMARY OR SECONDARY TEACHER?
As students get older, hormones kick in and some teenagers can be difficult to work with. Most primary teachers gave me the impression that it was much nicer to work with younger children. This may be so, but a primary school teacher has to deliver every subject. The work, planning, marking, recording, reporting that a primary teacher does is monstrous.

After eight years as a carpenter and joiner, married to Lin and now with children Stephen and Natalie, I am not really sure why I thought of teaching. Christmas, spring and summer holidays are always the fallback line as to why become a teacher. As well as securing regular pay and making our family's future more stable, it was the thought of doing some good, passing on knowledge to others, leading by example.

So, taking the bull by the horns, I phoned my local education office. "I would like some information on becoming a Design and Technology teacher please."

"Do you have English and Maths 'O' levels?"

"Yes."

"Do you have 'A' levels?"

"No."

"Well, I am sorry, but you cannot become a teacher."

I could have left it there, but it did not sit right with me. Just a gut feeling that the information was not correct. So I called again and spoke to someone different.

"Is it true that you need 'A' levels to teach?"

I got my answer: "No, as long as you have an advanced qualification relating to the subject you want to teach." Sorted, my advanced City & Guilds did the trick.

R1 asked me the question, "Why do you want to become a teacher?" After a tour of the DT facilities at Thames Polytechnic in Greenwich, R1, one of the lecturers, quizzed me. So I duly stated about setting a good example, passing on knowledge, looking after youngsters etc, etc. To be honest, I think I could have said the three holiday routine. As now, student equals funding. I was in, qualifications all good, no criminal record: teacher training was on.

4 Teacher training

So I started teacher training at Thames Polytechnic in September 1991. By the time I completed the two-year course of Bachelor of Education in Design and Technology, it had morphed into the University of Greenwich, so I was lucky enough to attend university!

Somehow we managed financially over those two years. As DT was short of subject teachers, I got a small grant. Lin was working two jobs and the odd bit of chippy work fed us all. With both sets of grandparents able to help out with childcare duties, we got through until my first appointment.

J1, R1, J2, R2 and M were the lecturers at uni. J1 was the all energetic and action-led lecturer. "Don't go maverick" was his famous catchphrase. Referring to working on your own assignments, the meaning was to keep in touch with your tutor to make sure you were heading in the right direction. Always enthused, he made you tired just listening and watching.

R1 was the next man down. A nice, relaxed fellow, the 'Hugh Laurie' of the lecturers, dealing with electronics. J2 and R2 would deal with the graphics. R2 was always a bit grumpy.

M was the computer whizz. He would set us programming tasks to complete without too much input. He had written part of the programmes and we had to finish them to suit our projects, with very little or no help. Self-learning: Ofsted would love it now.

To complete my degree, there were design/technology assignments, teaching practices and theory exams on teaching psychology/methods. With these courses inevitably comes a book list. I have never been a great reader. I will pick up books, check the size of font and see how many pictures are in it before I read it. If I am fortunate enough to get these thoughts published, I will go for a large font and try out my artistic skills. Fortunately, my children are all better readers. Those bedtime stories by Mum. I preferred playing table football with them instead!

The best part of teacher training, other than meeting fellow students, was the teaching practices. For if you cannot handle, like or enjoy those initial placements, then do not teach! I had one primary placement and three secondary schools.

The lectures were always a bit dry, dealing with equal opportunities and the theories of teaching. There was always a 'clever' student who could quote some great writer on their theory of teaching. Really just complicating common sense.

On my first placement at primary school, feeling 'clever', I asked the class teacher a question from my theory lectures about a 'model' learner. She did not have a clue as to what I was asking and, on reflection, neither did I! So from then on, I kept things simple.

My secondary school placements were enjoyable. I was keen, did all my prep, kept detailed files, lesson plans, schemes of work and observations. During my short time at the schools, I got involved with other aspects of school life, mainly sport. It certainly helped build relationships and respect. It helps manage that 'student teacher' in the classroom. It does not take long for a class to work out what and who you are. Similar to a supply teacher and not their normal teacher, if characters in a class want to be difficult, they will not care or think anything of you and you will just get one hell of a time.

Only once did this happen on my placements: my final day after six weeks at an all-boys' school in Tooting. Yes, it took them six weeks to work out that I was a student teacher and, as such, had no authority. I might add, it was not all students, just two or three who wanted to make my life difficult because they could. The majority were respectful and indeed wished me well when they left. More good than bad, a positive from a tricky last lesson.

After my two years teacher training, passing my exams, assignments and teaching practices, I passed and achieved my B.Ed in Design Technology. It was now onto finding my first post/appointment. This indeed would prove to be interesting and eye-opening.

5 Teaching interviews

As a newly qualified teacher (NQT), I applied for many posts initially. I found the process very strange indeed.

Many were just the schools going through the motions, seeing to be fair. There were several posts of Design Technology vacant, but I lost count of the times that the various schools employed a teacher who had been working on a temporary contract, or who had fulfilled a teaching practice there. Why on earth it was deemed necessary to waste three, four, five and, on one occasion, six other people's time is still a mystery.

All of the early interviews in 1993 required the candidates for the job to be there at the same time. A tour of the school and a special look at the Design Tech department facilities. Interviews followed, one candidate at a time, with candidates waiting and returning to an allocated room. Whilst the decision was being made, candidates would wait together. Once decided, the 'winner' would be called out and if it was not you, you knew you were not successful. (Unless the winner had a change of heart at the death.) The lead interviewer would then pop back in and say, 'Thanks, but no thanks.'

To negate a rejection of employment, the first question would be, 'If offered the appointment, would you accept?' Only once did I say 'No' and withdraw from the interview. That particular school were assessing their assessing of each pupil and then doing more assessing. Far too complicated, far too much for DT. The early days of the National Curriculum sent panic waves through schools; at least that's the impression I got.

My successful NQT interview saw me appointed at Burtona High School in Croydon. I was the pick of four candidates who were interviewed in May for a September 1993 start. Maybe the other three withdrew? Leaving only muggins! The issue with my appointment was one of salary. The head did not want to take my trade knowledge as experience and started me on the basic salary. My first battle was to get this experience acknowledged and my salary point notched up. This was the start of many unseen battles coming up at Burtona.

The interview process for a teacher has changed now. It now involves teaching a lesson to a class on a given topic by the school. After the formal interview, you leave and are contacted at a later time or date to inform you of your fate. Better than sitting in a room waiting to be told no.

My latest interviews in educational establishments have come about due to relocation. I have interviewed at schools and further education establishments. Again, usually a very quick tour, teaching and interview.

I have nailed the lid on the coffin of my secondary teaching career, after some bizarre interviews. One establishment wanted a construction teacher. They appointed a carpenter with no teaching qualification. Nothing against the gent but please, why ask me to attend if all you want to do is save money? I say money, because now age and experience are against me. Naturally I expect to be at the top end of the pay scale. I have worked hard to get there and work hard wherever I am. Another school got me to complete the DT GCSE exam from that summer. Mmmmmmmmm?

My final school interview involved being kicked out after teaching my lesson. I didn't even make the interview. "You're not what we are looking for." Still, I picked up on that when the head of department had asked me if I had a laptop? "No," was my answer and she did not raise a smile to me after that, so the writing was on the wall. Aside to this, though, the Year Seven pupils were lovely and came up with some good ideas to a rubbish topic set. RIP my secondary school teaching career, 1993-2013.

One of my latest interviews in further education for a carpentry and joinery lecturer was not successful due to the fact that they did not like my interview. However, my teaching session was good. The job was going to be re-advertised and due to the strength of my teaching, I could reapply for the position. It took the college eight weeks to get back to me from the initial interview. I replied that I was pleased that they thought my teaching was good, but felt that I could not offer anything new regarding my interview style.

Teaching interviews can be very strange.

6 Burtona High School

MY FIRST APPOINTMENT

Burtona was a mixed comprehensive school in the Borough of Croydon. It had a cohort of around nine hundred pupils from Years Seven to Eleven, and a large ethnic mix.

It had lovely grounds. As soon as you turned into the entrance gate, left took you to the staff car park, with ample parking for a change. On the right lay vast, lush grass playing fields being big enough to take three football pitches. A further pitch lay at the back of the school.

The one-level school buildings were in two blocks, A and B. In a previous life it had been an RAF hospital. Each block was the same shape. One corridor, that sloped in parts, feeding to another three corridors on the right-hand side. These corridors led to the classrooms on each side, or in RAF days, the wards. Off the main corridors to the left also lay other rooms which housed the gym suite, music, DT workshops, toilets, offices and storage cupboards in both blocks. At the bottom end, the blocks were linked by an icy covered walkway, scene of many a scrap. The top parts of the corridor were linked by the dining hall.

The main hall lay at the top of A block next to the school

reception and head's office. The school gym was situated at the top of B block. A tarmac playground divided both blocks at the top end. I have not been back in over twenty years, but I know that the school was razed to the ground and a new academy built.

As an NQT, we had to attend regular meetings with our mentor, supervisor J. As Burtona had its fair share of difficult students, being a non-selective comprehensive, many of the meetings discussed ways of classroom management and pupil behaviour. One such video I recall was regarding the 'check' or 'tick' on the board method. A teacher from the 70s, in his Lionel blares and perm hairstyle, demonstrated on a small group of adult learners trying to misbehave. Misdemeanours by a student would be marked with a check on the board. Each check equivalent to a punishment. So the first may be a warning check, then an extension of the lesson for that pupil, eventually leading to a detention, say, if three checks are achieved.

The trouble being, Burtona pupils loved getting their checks on the board. The more the merrier! I most likely will keep returning to the point, but I learnt quickly to develop my own methods, my own style to control behaviour. More often than not, it involved just discussion and respect for each other; being yourself. Some pupils never come around. The majority, however, do.

The most frustrating thing about those NQT meetings every month or two was the timing. J, our mentor, an experienced and excellent teacher, always had the meetings well planned and thought out. The free sandwiches always went down well. Some of the meetings coincided with important school events...football matches. So, rather than getting involved in other aspects of school life, showing another side of caring through my character as a referee or coach at an internal house match or fixture versus another school, I had to sit in a room and talk teaching. Those early meetings frustrated me. Don't get me wrong, it is important to talk to each other. But what works for me may not work for you. What works for you will be determined by your personality.

Student behaviour was poor at Burtona, especially in my second and third years there. After my first year the sitting headmaster left. He had strong control over pupils and staff. He was not liked by some staff, but pupils feared and respected him. He had control of events, backed up by a good deputy. C, 'the bill' (a TV series, for those of you that are too young to get that reference!), would be the enforcer, the face of discipline. There were softer, older, more compassionate members of staff also, who used their experience well. The mix kept Burtona ticking along. Future Ofsted would declare not, but I will deal with Ofsted later. Like lemmings, behaviour went over the cliff edge when the new head started. He was a softer character, but unfortunately he lost some of his staff from day one, as well as some of the pupils, too.

His first mistake came in the staffroom, a meeting with all staff members. A prepared speech on filing cards gave little feeling of his personality or vision. Indeed, when one card revealed that he had been pre-warned by the outgoing head that some staff had not been supportive of him, it alienated many.

By the time I left two years later, he had lost control of the school. Punishments for poor behaviour were not strong enough, with little consequence. The naughty pupils learnt this quickly and the plague spread down the ranks. Maybe the headmaster's hands were tied? Perhaps he couldn't expel too many pupils because of finance? If a head teacher cannot exert his/her authority over the pupils, there is Bob Hope and no hope for the teaching staff. Even C 'the bill' deputy lost his authority due to this.

An upper-school assembly demonstrated this fact. When the students fail to respond to a respectful, clear instruction to listen and stop talking whilst being addressed, instead talking over a senior member of staff, then the pupils are lost. Lost, because the bad eggs were ruling the roost.

There were attempts to rectify the situation. One came in the form of points, like on a driving licence. The theory was that any misdemeanour would be recorded and marked down: a paper-based system at the time. Forgetting equipment, one point; lateness, two points; swearing, three points. When a certain number of points were reached it would be detention time, letters home, internal exclusion, and eventually temporary or external exclusion.

It did not work. Firstly, the job of the collating was put on the one tutor. Twenty-five students to keep track of. Secondly, many of the teachers were too rigid, unable to see common sense. With punishment, you do not need to alienate good pupils. Some of my nicest, most well-behaved pupils came to me with points.

"What's this point for, Ashley?"

"I arrived slightly late to lesson."

"Why?"

"I was speaking with my teacher from the previous lesson."

"Did you explain?"

"Yes, but I still got a point."

"Ok, will file it, then."

"Thank you, sir."

"Leon, what's this for?"

"Forgot one ingredient for my food tech."

"What was that?"

"A spoonful of olive oil."

"Filed!"

Even the more difficult students received points for minor issues, all filed, respectively. Don't get me wrong: if a point was deserved, or the incident serious enough, it would be recorded. I took those decisions because it became a logistic nightmare. Points came at me thick and fast, too fast for my liking. The system, although a good thought, didn't take into account that some staff forgot about humanity. I always liked to look after my students, especially my tutor group. If a student forgets a piece of equipment, lend it to them: it saves a lot of hassle. After all, as teachers are we never late or do we never forget things?

Ultimately it failed because there was no end punishment. The ultimate of permanent exclusion didn't occur enough. With a system not delivering a final sanction, there is no system. How to address these issues in teaching, then? Have a meeting about them. We can discuss what we said in the last meeting, or discuss what we should discuss in the next meeting. Better still, let's get some external agencies to discuss issues we already know.

One such meeting at Burtona involved all staff, including the head discussing ethnic mix and behavioural issues within the school. An outside speaker preaching to us about things we could explain better to them. A point many in the room were muttering under their breath. Then came my 'Oliver Twist' moment. Raising my hand, getting the nod, I spouted along these lines.

"We know all this. The point being, if there are no ultimate sanctions for bad behaviour and the head teacher cannot control the students, there is little or no hope for the rest of us."

Although it was only my third year of teaching, I had some life experience. Coming from industry, with my own young family, I tell it how it is and still do. Many senior staff felt the same, but wouldn't have said it so publicly. I did have sympathy for the head teacher, however. I am sure there were politics of the situation that he did not relay to us, but he was the wrong candidate for that job. In the summer term of my final year at Burtona, the head met with every individual member of staff in his office.

"Are you going or staying at the end of term?" was his question.

"Going," was my reply. I returned to work on the tools and it would be six years before I returned to the classroom.

Even then, some teachers are far too full of their self-importance. Whilst waiting outside for an assembly to finish, the head of art asked, "Have you heard the news?"

"No," expecting some big revelation.

"I am leaving at the end of term."

"So am I!"

I am not sure if he wanted a salute or shoes polishing, but please don't get too up yourself when you gain the authority of being a teacher. Keep it real.

The most important measure for me was my tutor group. They were sad that I was leaving them and provided me with some good luck cards. I took heart in the fact that I had made a difference to some.

7 Willy

DO YOU GO HOME AND CRY?

Willy was a Year Ten student in one of my first GCSE classes at Burtona. It was a very difficult class with many difficult characters. Due to their behaviour, Willy asked me one lesson, "Do you go home and cry about us? We'll make you leave." This made me realise that some of the students were actually setting out to give me a difficult time.

Unless an incident is really dangerous or outrageous, as a teacher you must learn to deal with situations and handle the class. Take some 'flack' along the way, but deal with things. Educational theorists give you examples of good practice, but in reality you must develop a way of managing each group. It is purely personal as to how you do it. In Willy's case, I met fire with fire.

On one occasion I tossed his schoolbag up around fourteen feet, aiming for a ventilation duct at the top of the workshop. Unfortunately it missed narrowly and Willy claimed the bag back. Was it immature of me, not setting a good example? Yes, but it gave Willy the message that I would not be broken. Classes like that do take it out of you, but always leave them at work where they belong.

Indeed, about two months in, Willy and another classmate requested to leave and do another subject. I had won, but in reality it is probably what they wanted anyway, a way out from GCSE DT.

So I learnt that every child would not like doing DT, nor would every child like me. But most importantly, I learnt not to take it to heart.

In response to Willy's question, "Do you go home and cry?" No. Never.

8 Azir

THE BURNING BLAZER

I must have been crazy to attempt brazing (welding) with the difficult and disruptive Year Ten class, especially as it was a lesson observation as part of my initial NQT training / probation. Letting them loose with welding equipment did not go well. They were one of my few groups who did not enjoy practical work. It should have been a show-and-tell session with theory work. Not very good for their learning but safer at the time.

After my initial demonstration of how to weld on the hearth and going through the safety aspects which must be followed, the students were to take it in turns to braze. Before brazing, the metal had to be filed and cleaned. This could be done whilst waiting to use the hearth. A simple bracket was being produced as part of the knowledge syllabus.

With around sixteen students' needs to cater for, the plan to supervise the hearth and view the others whilst doing so hit problems. Helping across the workshop, Azir decided not to put an apron on. However, he also left his blazer on whilst at the hearth. In doing so, his blazer pocket came into contact with the head of the hot torch. Luckily, the flame was not on and he did not get burnt, but his blazer definitely needed a patch. According to Azir, it was done deliberately by another pupil.

The parents made a complaint regarding the blazer and that class never touched the brazing hearth again. The lesson observation paperwork was filed accordingly with 'needs improvement!'

It certainly aided future workshop management but, even so, accidents still occur with students not thinking or listening to instructions.

9 Stewart

THE DOWEL FIGHT

When there are around twenty students in a disruptive group, getting their attention can be difficult at times. On such occasions a loud, short, sharp bang often did the trick. To keep control some teachers have tried whistles. Others shout, or stand in silence. In reality, until you have developed a relationship with a group, you respect each other and the group know your expectations, group listening can be problematic, especially if you have difficult characters who do not want to be in your lesson. It all takes time.

I shouted many times at Burtona. In the short term it works, but in the long term it is no good for anyone. Roaring out at the class at least gets it off your chest. At times I resorted to using an 18mm piece of dowel, only short in length, to bang on the centre of the bench to gain attention. The benches at the time were hollow underneath for storage, with a lift-off centrepiece to gain access. This made a magnificent, loud 'bang' with a stick.

Stewart, a Year Nine student, thought it would be a good idea to move his hand back and forth on the centre of the bench as I struck it. I would strike the bench no more than three times. Anymore and I think I would have been losing the plot. Well, you guessed it. As the dowel travelled down at velocity for the final time, Stewart misjudged his co-ordination and left his hand in the centre of the bench! Needless to say, the dowel made perfect contact across the back of his hand. Stewart didn't move from his seat the whole lesson, he didn't do any work, and he remained quiet.

I had apologised because it certainly was not deliberate, just unfortunate. Stewart did not take my apology well. Upon leaving at the end of the lesson, Stewart grabbed his own piece of dowel. Luckily for me it was only 10mm thick, but quite long. Stewart lunged at me, striking me three times across the top of the body. Before his fourth attempt I managed to grab hold of him, remove the dowel from his grasp and pin him to the wall of the workshop.

"Do you want to go for it, then?" I requested.

"No," was the answer.

I did not complete any behaviour reports or refer Stewart. It was a situation of my own making and I probably deserved what I got in return. Stewart was fine the next lesson he had DT. As a teacher you cannot hold any grudges, despite how difficult some students may be.

10 Perry

B S

BS stood for Behavioural Support, paperwork that would be completed on a student after an unacceptable incident. If it was deemed very serious, the student could end up in the behavioural unit/room. Basically, it was the 'naughty room'. Like supernanny's naughty step, a place to go, reflect, work and receive support for their issues. Every school has one, or a behavioural policy to follow.

I wrote a BS form on Perry, a diminutive Year Seven student. When I requested he do something towards his work, he responded to me, "You're a fucking idiot and a lanky wanker."

On the BS form, I stated that I agree with the idiot and lanky, but object to the rest.

Twenty-five years later, I think Perry was right!

Woodwork

11 Chesney

Chesney was of African background. A Year Eleven student, medium-height but slim and slender with a brilliant smile. A cheeky chap, who thought he was good at DT, but didn't work hard enough.

At Burtona, I was also given the task of taking the same group for computer studies. The work would be set by the IT teacher and I would 'babysit' the lesson, attempting to deal with any questions with my limited IT skills at the time. One such question arose about the server and its memory storage. A good server around then was Boris Becker, I thought? It was not a comfortable lesson in the early days of IT, considering I was still learning myself.

At the end of one of these classes, I stood up from the front of the desk, easing my chair away behind me. Then, dismissing the students and overseeing their exit from the same position, with no issues I went to sit back down on my chair. Only my chair was gone. Chesney had slipped behind me and removed it. As I fell arse over tit on the floor, there stood Chesney with his chalky-white grin, thinking he was funny. The other students who saw gasped and awaited my reaction.

Jumping to my feet, Chesney was the next person off his feet. I had pinned him to the whiteboard with my left forearm. Placing my face closer to his, I said quietly, "It's lucky you are only a boy."

In all of my teaching years, this was the closest I have come to striking a student, for what was an idiotic piece of behaviour. I didn't do, or need to do, a behaviour form: Chesney was quite clear about what would happen if he tried future pranks. The issue had been dealt with, and the majority of times, as a teacher, you have to find a way of dealing with issues and just get on and do it.

12 Bushwaka

I was called 'Bushwaka' by a Year Ten DT student who found it difficult to understand that I sharpened pencils using a chisel. Each time it brought him out in a fit of hysterics: "Why not use a sharpener?" he'd laugh.

Well, I explained, as a chippy onsite, you do not carry a pencil sharpener. You use your tools, especially if you are using a carpenter's pencil for stud or roof work. I have always been a tradesman at heart.

Needless to say, he never got the point, or took the opportunity to sharpen his pencil with a chisel.

Bushwaka and a giggle were always his main priorities. Still, it kept him happy in a difficult class.

13 Carlton Boys

After six years in exile from teaching, I returned to teach at the school I attended as a boy. By chance really, Lin had seen the advert in the local council newsletter and brought it home. At the time I was a uniformed police officer and on the verge of transferring services to earn more money. I enjoyed being a uniformed officer: helping people was my main aim. Understanding, being considerate, arresting and issuing tickets only as a necessity, not obligatory. To look after and keep people safe, as I would expect other officers to do for my family. For some, it was not like that, but again authority goes to some heads and affects people in strange ways. After a couple of years, the politics, workload and work life of an officer were proving difficult. Once you are a police officer, it becomes your life. Family, events, meetings...all get pushed aside.

So I applied for the position of DT teacher. Before the interview, I had a visit and met S, the head of DT, and Mr C the head. On that visit it felt like going home. In the long term Carlton had been good to me. However, it didn't start like that as a boy in the second year (Year Eight).

As a family we had moved from Lilleshall Road in Morden to a house in Carshalton. Of course, as an eleven, nearly twelve-year-old boy I didn't want to move. I loved Lilleshall Road, liked my middle school and had lots of good friends. In reality, it was only a couple of miles away, but it felt like a lot more at that age.

In my final year at middle school, I left in the April to start at Carlton Boys. My friends were all going to the local Merton high school, but my brother and sisters had not got on well there, so it was decided I would go to a different school.

As I was just about to start at Carlton Boys, the lower west wing was burnt down by a disgruntled student. It led to an extra week off before being thrown in at the deep end. I was now a small fish in a big pond. The school smelt like burnt baked beans because of the fire, and I was singled out by the bully because I was the 'newbie'. I hated those few months of the summer term. I missed Lilleshall and my old friends.

Life quickly changed for me at Carlton Boys in the autumn term. After a chat with Mum and contact with the school, Mr C sorted the bullying issue. For anybody who is being bullied, do not be afraid to speak out.

'Eggy', my maths teacher, moved me into the top set to get me away from another boy who had started at the school, but was refusing to adapt. Most importantly, staff and students alike realised that I could play football and was pretty good at other sports. Once in the school team, it gives you a certain kudos, ranking that you are appreciated by your peers. There were still others that I would avoid, but as a whole school became enjoyable again, all because I could play football. So in the end, Carlton Boys did well for me and that affection for the place will stay with me, because the teachers looked after and did their best for me.

To go back and teach at the school you went to as a child, however? It seemed a bit strange to some, but I felt like I needed to give something back to the school that had done well for me. So, after a successful interview, getting a better salary than my police pay, not having to work shifts or weekends, and having better family time, I returned to teaching. Little did I know that I would give Carlton Boys another eleven and a half years.

The main fabric of the building was the same. A curved centre section housed reception, school offices and head's room. At either end on two floors lay the west and east wings. Behind these lay the sixth-form block, the gym, and new science and art blocks. In my time teaching there, a new maths block was also built. Across the road lay the school sports field, where a new sports hall had been built. An astro pitch was also soon to be built, improving the facilities further. However, the most important aspect of the school was not the buildings being added to it, but the ethos of the place. The ethos of caring, wanting the best for its pupils, not just in an academic sense. There are probably Carlton Boys out there who may disagree that the place did well for them, but the majority I have met again seem of the same opinion as me.

14 Homework

In my workshop at Carlton Boys, I made a poster and stuck it above the double doors which led to the machine shop/ tech room.

For the poster I drew a fish, A3 in size. I coloured the fish red and called it the homework fish. Many students asked me about it, but only one came up with the answer. It was a red herring.

A red herring, because far too much importance and emphasis are placed on homework. After a long, hard day at work, what do you want to do when you get home? Oh yes, start working again!

We all have a lifetime of work ahead of us and school is only a short period of our lives. The majority work really hard at school, so out of school children should be having fun at the park, finding their own interests, socialising face to face with each other, playing sport, developing life skills. Avoid too much computer and computer game use. Most of the above is also done at after-school clubs and sports fixtures. Just give them the chance to be young and have fun before the real world kicks in. Children are under too much pressure too early in their lives.

Would I ban homework? No. But I would make it optional. Supply it only for those that want some.

15 Jock

Jock was a large unit for his age. A Year Eleven student. Not the brightest, but a nice fella and a GB judo champ in his age group. This somewhat gave him a false sense of invincibility. Nobody could defeat him in a judo or wrestling match.

Although I was slightly taller, Jock had the greater weight advantage and was physically strong. I am not sure how it arose, but he made me a challenge that I could not get out of his headlock once he had hold. Naturally, I accepted.

Jock made his headlock from the side, wrapping his right arm around my neck, clasping it with his left arm and pulling me tight into the side of his waist. Fortunately, he had not gone for the rear headlock!

As he did this, I turned my neck so that I could breathe and there was no pressure on the blood vessels running down the side of the neck. Jock is now squeezing hard, but has both hands tied up, I have both hands free.

With a crowd of onlookers and just about to make my move, the deputy head waltzes in. In his broad Cornish accent asks, "What's going on in here, then, Mr Clark?"

The onlookers appeal, "It's alright, sir, it's a challenge." I confirm that I am ok and with the pincer movement of my left hand in the correct position, from my police training, Jock quickly lets go!

As with any physical challenge activity, never underestimate your opponent. You do not know anyone's background or capability. Better still is to avoid all physical contact and sort issues out verbally...discuss and resolve.

16 Leroy

As part of the construction course, I would arrange site visits through a Wates contact. The Wates staff also visited some of the lessons at school to talk with the students. As well as this, when new buildings were being erected on the school site, the contractors would come and talk to the construction students. As part of one course, we also did a first aid qualification for the students.

For me, it was great. These were real-life situations, scenarios and jobs being discussed in the workshop-classroom situation. The visits always went down well with cross-curricular links, a subject that was big at the time. Moreover, the students also enjoyed escaping from school for a day.

Before one site visit, I was explaining to the group what we were going to see and view. Also the links to English and Maths in terms of communication, paperwork and calculations involved. One member of the group raised his hand.

"Yes, Leroy?"

"What's Maths got to do with construction?" he asked.

For some, there is no help.

17 Dave

Schools often have internal or external activities for students who are struggling or having difficulty in certain areas of their lives or learning. Once such activity was called 'Building Bridges'.

Dave, a Year Eleven student at the time, who in today's society would be classed as clinically obese, would often miss some lessons to attend the group.

One such lesson was an IT lesson taught by Mr W. Mr W was my old woodwork teacher when I was a student and he had a wicked sense of humour. Indeed, Mr W was disappointed with me as a student, because I went down the CSE route as I struggled with English and wanted to put more time into that subject. (My decision was vilified as I passed my English 'O' level and achieved a grade one in woodwork, worth another 'O' level. Hey, I wasn't too bad at woodwork then!)

Mr W was calling the register for the group.

"Dave?" he called.

"He is at Building Bridges, sir," another student replied.

"Building Bridges? More like he should be at testing bridges!" Mr W retorted.

18 Luke

In my near nineteen years of being in teaching, this incident was the worst I had to deal with. If I had known the student, or taught him before this, it wouldn't have happened. As I had no relationship with him, it all kicked off, big time!

I had just taken my Year Ten enrichment sports lesson over at the sports field. Walking back down to my workshop in the lower east wing corridor, there was a skirmish between three boys, nothing unusual in a boys' school.

However, this was slightly different. Luke had another student in a headlock and it didn't look too friendly or playful. Luke was a Year Nine student but, for his age, taller and stronger than most in his year group.

As always, I started with a simple request, knowing that any hold around the neck is potentially very dangerous.

"Let him go please."

Nothing, totally ignored.

With over one thousand pupils within the school, I didn't yet know these three.

"Let him go," I repeated.

Nothing, ignored again.

I took Luke by the lapels of his blazer with both hands

and pulled him off the assault. Luke looked at me, incensed.

"Take your fucking hands off me."

"Calm down and I will."

"Take your fucking hands off me," Luke repeated.

The incident was now creating a little noise and attention, but there was no way I was letting go until he stopped swearing and calmed down.

"Calm down," I replied again.

"Take your fucking hands off me!"

We had now been joined by S, the head of DT, a little concerned with the incident.

"I will email SMT (Senior Management Team) to get someone down here. Perhaps take him into the workshop out of view to calm down?" he said.

We were just outside N's workshop. N, another DT teacher, was a good teacher but always a little disorganised. As it was lunchtime, with no students or class in the workshop, it should have been a better environment. However, as Luke and I grappled into the room, N had not got his previous class to tidy away and, subsequently sitting on the first bench lay scissors and Stanley knives. Luke and I had now reached a stalemate. He was not calming down and I was not going to let him go until he did.

With a swift move, I released one hand to push all the objects off the bench and onto the floor so that it was out of reach. Luke, seizing the opportunity, struggled further to release my one hand.

"Take your fucking hand off me!"

Unable to break free, I took the decision to put Luke in a position where I could contain him more safely, laying him on his back across the bench. This only proved to further enrage him, but there was no way I was letting go. He was challenging my authority.

"Calm down and I will," I repeated.

"Take your fucking hands off me, you donkey-shagging cunt!"

I was not going to let go, but I made sure the force I used was not excessive, not striking him or holding him in a dangerous position, so as to ensure that he could breathe!

S was getting a little uptight with the situation. SMT had not appeared and I do not think that any of the DT teachers that S had worked with would handle the situation the way I was.

"Let go, you donkey-shagging cunt!" Luke shouted again.

"Calm down and I will."

Now, totally frustrated that he could not break free, Luke upped the ante. As I leaned over him, he started to spit, aiming at my face. Like a November 5th firework, a steady stream of gob heading upwards. (Fortunately not real 'greenies'!) Some caught me in the face, but I was like Will Smith in *Men in Black 3*: Will, on the launch pad, avoided the bullets from the baddy by ducking and diving. He went back in time to achieve it, but I had no such luxury.

As I shimmed and swayed my head like a boxer avoiding a punch, the gob that missed started its return flight. It missed me on the way down and started to catch Luke in his own face. Sucker punches, making him blink also. So now Luke was struggling, gobbing and blinking, as well as still swearing at me.

"Let go, you donkey-shagging cunt!"

"Calm down and I will."

SMT in the shape of Mr W then arrived. W, the Head of PE at the time, was a great personality and well liked by students and staff alike.

"Alright, Luke?" he asked.

"Yes, sir," Luke replied.

Luke had instantly calmed. I released my grip and Luke headed off with W. I headed off to my sink to clean off the spit which had hit the target.

Luke had calmed down because he had already developed a relationship with W. They knew each other, and that goes a long way in teaching. I, too, now had a relationship with Luke. We knew what each other was about.

At the start of Year Ten, Luke turned up to my construction lesson. A lesson he had picked as one of his choices. Full of chisels, knives, saws etc. Standing with a big grin across his face, Luke asks, "Remember me?"

"Yes, Luke, how are you?" I replied with a big grin back.

The good thing about boys, they tend not to hold grudges.

As a teacher, you must not either. Our relationship started in a poor way, but it had begun. Until that relationship is developed – and sometimes it can take a while – you cannot teach.

Sadly for Luke, he had other issues around school and did not make it to Year Eleven. I had no further problems with him. Indeed, he used to work well in construction when he was there.

19 Zane

Zane. The 'wood banger' who had issues. He became known as the wood banger by me and the rest of the construction group. Whilst attempting certain woodwork joints, if they went wrong or not to plan, Zane would take his timber and give it a serious workout on the bench, banging it with all his might.

We all stood back, let him get on with it and, once finished, I would ask:

"Problem, Zane?"

As a teacher, I did not know the full ins and outs of Zane's issues. What was his upbringing like? How about his home life?

As a teacher, person, whatever, do not judge. Some pupils lead very extreme lives out of school. All you can do is look after and help them whilst they are with you for that short time.

Sadly, Zane did not finish his schooling at Carlton Boys.

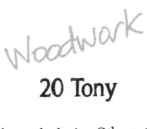

Woodwork

20 Tony

Tony suffered from dyslexia. Other students also did, amongst other learning infringements. Most would work hard and try their best, despite their struggles. Tony thought it was an excuse not to work or try.

In one construction theory lesson, Tony had failed to do any work and was not attempting to either. I strolled over, 'helicoptering' around the room. Often in teaching, new words or techniques would be put in place to describe activities that have gone on in the classroom since time had begun. Hence helicoptering, meaning walking around the room to see what is going on.

Practical lessons always involved being mobile. Such lessons operate differently to theory subjects, as do the skills and techniques required, a point lost on some theorists.

"Not working today, Tony? Don't tell me, it's because you're dyslexic?"

Tony complained and I had to meet with him and the teaching support team. I had made Tony feel bad and humiliated in front of the class and, as a result, I was requested to apologise, which I duly did.

His classmates knew the score. They knew he was using

it as an excuse not to work and they knew me.

"He was bang out of order, sir," one student commented.

21 Knighthood?

I never once insisted that a student call me Sir. After all, I had not been knighted, and am never likely to be. It is just a mark of respect that, as a child you offer the teacher.

I was happy with Mr Clark, or Mr C, especially at Carlton Boys. During their final term in Year Eleven, as the boys were leaving, to many I just became 'Clarky', especially among my tutor groups.

After five years with them, most were leaving as friends.

22 Head teachers

When I went into teaching, the purpose for me was to have direct contact with the students, to teach. I had no grand ambitions to climb the ladder to headship because, once on that trail, you start to become a manager, teach less, and lose contact with the classroom. I have worked under three heads and I will not include the heads of the schools during my teaching practices.

Similar to a football referee, the head's position is a difficult one. They are well paid, but I would not want it. Although, having said that, I did qualify as a referee for a period of time, before I got fed up with the overgrown 'has-beens' thinking they were the best thing since sliced bread.

You can please most some of the time, but not all, all of the time. Every head had staff who liked or disliked them, depending on their dealings with them.

Mr A, my first head at Burtona, had more staff who disliked him. However, he had control of the school. Other than a battle to raise my starting salary as my first appointment, I had no issues with him. I did not see him much and did not need to.

Mr B took over from Mr A at Burtona and unfortunately,

as explained previously, it did not go well for him. Now I can empathise with him, but in essence he was not ruthless enough with the students. He knew that because I publicly stated it, rather than talk behind his back like some others. It was never personal, always professional, and I had no issues with talking to him.

On a traditional basis, I have always liked (and still do) to talk differences out face to face. Not in memos, emails, texts, or even phone calls. If you have got a problem with someone or something, sort it face to face. Be honest.

Mr C at Carlton Boys was the head teacher I worked under for the largest amount of time. During that time, he took the school from local authority control to academy status, producing good results. It also enabled a promotion to Principal for him!

On my pre-interview visit to Carlton Boys, I met Mr C for the first time. It was around the time of his second year at Carlton Boys after taking over from 'Beefy', the previous head, an old deputy when I was a boy at the school. Mr C was down to earth and had visions of how he wanted to improve the school and take it further. I always got on well with him and still do to this day. Others I know saw his ruthless side. Some members of the DT department were rumoured to have been offered terms to leave.

Mr C was never like that with me. He always looked after me, salary-wise and emotionally. I will always hold him dear for the way he treated me when my dad died.

He looked after me well. I like to think it was because I was a good teacher at Carlton Boys. Being an ex-pupil I knew where the boys were coming from and I did not take it too seriously or to heart if someone did not want to play ball. I did other things out of the workshop to add value to the place: cycle club, darts, football, woodwork club, bike maintenance, even an Arsenal championship winning party.

Before my leaving speech Mr C requested, "Make us laugh." So I duly did. Sadly, I think I upset him because some comments regarding teaching methods hit too close to the bone. Other staff could see the funny side.

Still, as with all of my previous work colleagues and friends, if he needs my help at anytime in the future, he only has to ask. As a fellow Gooner, I duly will.

23 Other staff

The most important staff who work at schools are not the teachers, although many will disagree.

Firstly, there are the cleaners. If the school is not cleaned well you cannot teach.

The site team keep the school in motion, so treat them well. The chef and canteen or (cafe) staff who feed the troops. The brilliant support staff. The office and admin staff, the unsung heroes within a school. The untold work and pressure they are under is ridiculous. If you do not have good office staff, the school is in trouble. I take my hat off to them all.

Of course, you need good teachers, but some get above their station, lose sight of whom and what you are dealing with, and take life much too seriously.

As a police officer, it was a duty to make eye contact, smile and say hello. I continue to this day and, as a teacher, if a colleague or pupil was passing, I would smile and say hello. Not once did a pupil fail to respond. Many teachers walked straight past. Was it because I was underneath them? Some, maybe, but again most were too wrapped up in their own world. Their own pressures bearing down on them, planning, delivering, preparation, with the next lesson always on the horizon. Too busy to remember that others exist in this world and that a simple act of kindness is far more important.

The 'delegators' also made me laugh. These were teaching staff who came up with a bright idea that the management team liked. They would then pass this on to other teachers to do the work and prep for it. Once completed and successful, they would take the credit and a round of applause.

I was never bothered about rounds of applause at briefings. I didn't need clapping for doing my job. The croissants and coffee were more than enough if I made it in to partake, which was not often.

There have been many staff members over the years that I should thank for their help and support. Some more closely than others. But if you know me, thank you all. However, GDPR regulations mean that I will not name them personally.

A special mention does go out to my French brother and fellow Gooner, though: Ça va?

24 Tutor groups

As a group tutor, lots get dumped on you. Extra activities, ideas, and things to do which do not fit into the normal timetable get squeezed into tutor time.

From 'thought of the day', CV work, diary writing, homework planning, mentoring, extra maths, English: all and everything was attempted during tutor time.

Management always wanted it to be the start of learning for the day. Get the students in the right frame for learning by prepping for the day ahead. In reality, it all becomes too much and, if you tried to fit in everything that is wanted, you would drown, along with the students.

I took a different view to tutor time. It was a time to relax and talk to each other. For me to learn about the students and for them to discuss with each other. Communicating with others is an important aspect of learning.

Only once did I lose my rag in tutor time: during a structured activity the students failed to listen. A few tables and chairs flew that morning.

In extended tutor time I introduced word and maths games. Scrabble, Boggle, Word Up, Countdown, darts, and my personal favourite, table football. Nobody beat Mr C at table football. It was all valuable learning time, even if not formally recorded or assessed. The most important aspects of teaching are the unmeasurable things you do. The listening ear, the encouragement, the time given up to discuss or engage in extra activities.

One morning whilst playing darts with my Year Eleven tutor group, the head of year hauled me out of the class.

"I need these doing more in the morning than just playing darts."

"Well, Mr M, we are actually doing maths."

I took him back into the room and showed him our tutor group plan for the week, structured to use darts for Maths.

"How do you finish on 169?" I asked Mr M.

"Erm?"

"That's right, you can't."

"I will leave it with you," he said.

I got on well with my tutor groups, especially with the groups that I had for a few years. These groups left as my friends. I enjoyed the Year Eleven leaving party with my early groups. The tutor made a speech about their group and it was my time to take the 'Mick' and give it back to them with both barrels, which I certainly did. Those parties-events turned into Year Eleven leavers' BBQ at Carlton Boys with very few speeches or 'Mickey-taking'. It was not the same. Some tutors did not want to make, or like making the speech, so it was just a general farewell from all. Dull to say the least.

25 Cover lessons

In my early years, if fellow teachers were absent, often you would be used for cover. If you had a free lesson (the time you had planned to do some marking or prep), you could get, and were often used, to take the lesson for that teacher.

I always dreaded viewing the cover sheet. Darn! On it again. We all fall ill from time to time and for genuine cases it was not an issue. Some staff names, though, continually cropped up as absent. What was done about it?...Nothing. If you are away as a teacher, it puts the workload on everyone else, so make it in if you can.

The other issue with cover was turning up and having no work set or planned. Have a backup plan; take some pencils just in case. My favourite maths backup plan was darts again. A drawing of a dartboard onto the whiteboard and a series of questions that followed. Adding, subtracting, dividing, multiplying. All come into play and it used to fill the lesson well. I even used it for one GCSE Year Eleven maths group and some struggled with it.

Most cover involved some form of worksheet, or finishing work from the previous lesson. The main priority in a cover lesson would be behaviour. As long as that is acceptable, any work done was a bonus. Do not make life hard in a cover lesson: they are lucky to have you there.

Cover did diminish, however. Cover assistants were employed by the school and it was their job to sit in for teachers who were away. Only in desperate times were you used. It was all to do with reducing the teacher's workload, allowing more prep time. Due to finances, this luxury, perhaps, may have disappeared now.

On my final day at Carlton Boys I was given a Year Eight English lesson to cover...great.

The only positive with a cover lesson is that it allows the students to see you in a different light, another side of you. It also allows you to see what they are up to out of your domain. Their quality of work and attitude. How does it compare with your lesson?

26 Ofsted, inspections and the Education Minister

Raise the alarm! Panic stations! Ofsted are coming! School is open late, till 9 tonight, over the weekend for you all to prepare.

This was the response in the early stages of Ofsted inspections. Many teachers would genuinely be afraid or worried about the forthcoming inspection. It was all about the quality of teaching, so we were under the microscope.

Ofsted would call a week in advance and inform the head that they would be attending. It gave the school that time to prepare, as well as a further week to panic. Inspectors would then observe lessons, inspect paperwork, give feedback and grade the school.

The grades have evolved over the years from excellent, good, satisfactory and requires improvement, to outstanding, good, satisfactory and special measures. What started as good is now a satisfactory and the Holy Grail for all is now outstanding. The advance warning time then reduced. Ofsted moved the call to a Friday afternoon – before 12 pm, to inform the school it would be inspected on the Monday, and yes, school was open late that night and on the Saturday. Ofsted should just turn up and see how the school really runs.

Anybody could come into my lesson, anytime they wanted. I always worked a certain way, structured the lesson how I wanted. I didn't do anything different during inspection time than I would do in a normal week. After all, who are inspectors? People like you and me. Teachers who had had enough of teaching or who maybe couldn't teach became inspectors.

I always took Ofsted with a pinch of salt. For me, they were judging schools on the wrong values. In the early days it was results: how many GCSEs and what grades? All to go into those sodding league tables. I was never bothered by league tables either. Not whilst teaching and not when considering schools for my own children.

Far more important for me was the ethos and the feeling of the school. How the school would look after and encourage my sons and daughter to work hard and be nice people. How they would help nurture them. Would they leave school being able to put the feelings of others before their own? Would they know that they had to work hard to survive and not be a burden to others? Be caring and show empathy to others? Of course, upbringing and home life should do this as well, but school should support and reinforce those values. These things are far more important to me than a piece of paper showing the number of GCSEs obtained. The issue was that school focused far too much on the GCSE results and this got hammered into the students as a result. Why? Because this is how the school is judged, on results.

So a student could work as hard as possible, do their best and achieve a grade D. Not a failure, but it sure felt like a fail because it was not the magic pass of a C and so it would affect the school's overall percentage. Results focused the student on me, me, me. It reminded me of the 1980s decade under Margaret Thatcher. Me, me, me. Greed, greed, greed. The 'yuppie' years.

If my teaching, my style, was not deemed good enough, or not appropriate, then it was no problem for me: get someone else to do it, then. For I am a tradesman and can drop back on the tools at anytime. I was a good teacher and happy to be a good teacher. I was rarely ill, kept on top of the paperwork, and made my students the priority. Ofsted and learning walks were always seeking good to outstanding. Always wanting you to improve, get better, and make the learning outstanding. I had a formula that worked. I was good, my lessons were good, and most importantly the majority of students enjoyed the lessons and their time with me.

Learning walks were completed by senior management, or those on the promotion ladder gaining a feel for inspection. You would be visited during any lesson, the pupils questioned for a short time whilst they were working. Again, no problem to me: it should have happened more often. As a practical teacher, it should have given the theorists an insight into how we work, what we have to deal with. Twenty Year Seven pupils with saws and chisels learning!

Ofsted evolved into focusing more on the learner. How was the student learning? How was the student making progress every lesson? How was the student taking control of his or her own learning? How was the teacher facilitating this?

Senior management would have all of the policies in place to inspect; teachers themselves would need to make sure schemes of work were in place and in the early years, lesson plans sorted.

In reality a good teacher does not need lesson plans to teach. When starting out, I can understand them, but after gaining experience you plan the lessons in your head. You have to be able to adapt during lesson if things are not going to plan. Some teachers stay at school to plan, produce lesson plans, schemes of work, set targets, goals. The majority of my planning I did on my bike. Whilst others stayed late, I went for a bike ride. On my bike I could relax, think about my next day, plan what I needed to do with the groups I would be teaching. I certainly didn't need to record everything down. I loved my bike, my bike was my office. It also helped me train for the charity bike rides I undertook.

Two inspections in particular stand out for me, and they were not by Ofsted. (My Ofsted inspections were always ok, satisfactory as a minimum.) The first was by a teacher recently promoted to senior management. Deep into the summer term, it was a DT lesson with a Year Nine group. With Year Nine having made their option choices, at least half of the group were not taking a DT option for their GCSE. Those not taking the subject were grouped on benches completing some isometric drawing. Independent learning! Others were doing work related to what DT aspect they were taking up in the forthcoming year. A theory lesson. I would float around the workshop, help out and advise if needed. The member of staff inspecting came in at the start of the lesson. I explained the situation and after ten minutes the member of staff declared, "I will come back at the end of the lesson to see some teaching."

The end of the lesson came and the SMT member duly came back in to see the plenary, which was, "Ok lads, well done. Books and equipment away please, sit down quietly ready to go."

The member of staff gave me a slating for this lesson. Again, it certainly did not bother me. That staff member had no idea of the context of the lesson and was not interested in my methods, or indeed if the students had behaved and worked well all lesson. The staff member was well out of their depth, a theorist inspecting an experienced practical teacher. Further pinches of salt required. There are more important things in life than inspections.

The second inspection that stands out was an external one. External inspections involved agencies being brought into your department to inspect your methods, teaching and learning. On one such occasion, SMT sent in a gentleman called Mr L. Mr L informed us of what a good teacher he was and how well he had taught DT at 'A' level. So he carried out his lesson observations on us all. On his final day of inspection, he sat in my workshop in discussion with another member of the DT team. He looked at me, said nothing and then left without even talking to me. I knew what was coming. On the Monday, I asked our head of department, "How did our inspection go?"

"Not well."

"What a surprise!"

Guess what? Mount Everest pinch of salt time. If someone cannot front you face to face, explain why they think you are rubbish, then their opinion does not matter. Some weeks down the line SMT did some further research into Mr L's observation techniques and discovered his main theories were full of holes, so that 'mini'-Ofsted on our department was filed. By the end of that term I received full vindication. My level 1 construction group achieved the best results for an English school at that level. A nice certificate adorned my workshop wall (in fact several took pride of place). A fellow DT disciple mentioned the fact of our results in briefing after slipping through SMT minds.

I did not need applause, I just needed to be trusted to do my job. In fact, I have not yet met one teacher who has not cared about what they do. We became teachers for a reason, worked hard to get there, so give us the professional courtesy and trust deserved.

The whole Mr L episode was about taking construction to level 2. Why? Level 2 could be counted in the school success figures. I was not to forget Mr L (I referred to him as the lion man). During many an input to the students, where I would be demonstrating a technique, I would say to the group, "The lion man would be pleased with that!" Totally over the students' heads, but our DT technician and I always had a good chuckle. Indeed, often I would sing the little ditty, "He's the lion man", just like the New Zealand TV programme. The students thought I was nuts, and they were correct.

THE EDUCATION MINISTER

Our famous Education Minister at the time was one reason I decided to leave secondary education. The *Daily Mail* reported on how well he was doing, shaking up education for the better. By now, I had taught hundreds of pupils and lessons alike. Here was a man taking advice from his peers, but never having taught a single lesson or group in his life. Please, if you have never stood up in front of a class for any period of time, do not tell me how to do my job.

According to the minister, school should start earlier,

finish later, have shorter holidays, coursework banned, the exam system changed and made harder. Well, Education Minister, if you had opened your eyes and looked properly you would have seen that much of that went on before you arrived on your lofty throne.

Before school there is breakfast club. During school, other than lessons, clubs and activities would be happening during break, lunch and after school. Then there are the many sports fixtures into the early evening. Not forgetting open evening, parents' evening and a swimming gala that would go beyond 9 in the night-time. How much later did he want school to carry on?

Teachers and students alike work really hard during term-time and so deserve the holidays to recharge. I believe the students especially need that time to relax and have fun. I know I did when I was young, enjoying the chance of more football or cycling. School still used to operate, though, with extra revision during Easter and summer school during August. The Education Minister did not look hard enough and that is because he had never worked in a school.

The minister decided that coursework would be chopped, made redundant and discarded as if meaningless, despite the hours of work put in by the students. His own government brought in coursework. The exams changed from A* to U to 9 to 1. Why not use A*, A and A- to denote the levels within a grade, which has been done since time had begun? At least people would have some idea of where they stand. Nobody has a 'scooby' at present which represents a pass. Four or five this year? Five and above next year? More students passing with good grades? Exams must be getting easier? Let's make them harder. Actually the students were working hard to achieve them.

So what should have happened? Every head teacher in the land should have stuck together and told the Education Minister what's what. Did it happen? Of course not. Obviously head teachers did not share my views. So, as in Dragons' Den, "I was out", for teaching.

What sort of man was the Education Minister? He would later campaign for Brexit. Once achieved, like all of the Brexiteers, he disappeared and left the poor Prime Minister to pick up the pieces. He would also stab a colleague in the back, seeking his own promotion.

That is the Education Minister who lost not only me, but I am sure also lots of other teachers from the profession.

As I left, one point stood out for me. A student whose native tongue was Spanish could cook the most fabulous Spanish dishes. 'À la carte', according to our food tech team. A*, 9 in value. Did he get his GCSE equivalent? No, because he could not write about it in English or understand fully the exam paper. Well, exam papers certainly taste nice when cooked well!

27 Unions

When you become a teacher, join a union. It is a must, a given. Not because you want to join the revolution, but for your own protection. A union will have your back whatever the situation, so subscribe. In terms of personal protection, a union is your goliath.

My only frustration with teaching unions is that there are too many of them. Too many for a combined sense of purpose. There is no unity between them.

I was a member of NASUWT. When requested to strike, the decision was not taken lightly, but I did because the union had declared that as a way of action. Even then, some teachers did not, as it was still personal preference. However, those teachers would also reap the effect if any benefits were claimed. Strikes were not effective anyway. NASUWT would strike one day, NUT another, so school was able to function. Sometimes in a reduced capacity, but still able to open.

When there was a serious conflict with government, teachers should have been like the London Underground drivers. If a strike was called, all teachers everywhere, up and down the land, in every single school should have walked out and refused to return to work until an acceptable settlement was reached. Chaos? Yes, it would have been, but I guarantee that the government would have resolved the issue within twenty-four hours. It would not have been like Scargill and the poor miners.

It would never happen, however.

In that respect, unions are spineless, not even fully supported by their own members.

28 Workshops

I made my workshops my domain, both at Burtona and Carlton Boys.

Burtona was a mess when I arrived. I duly stripped out, tidied and organised, much to the annoyance of the site manager. He complained about the rubbish I had created. He ultimately got the 'tin tack'. Not just my doing.

I put up displays of good work, sanded all the graffiti off the benches, recovered them, organised the room how I wanted it; generally, I tried to make it a nicer, neater place.

I went further at Carlton Boys. As well as good work, slogans, quotes, Arsenal memorabilia and old toys my children had grown out of were all on display. Dartboards were also on the wall for extra-curricular activities. It all provoked discussion and gave the students an insight into my personality. Fairy lights were strung around the top of the workshop and turned on through December. I renamed the workshop 'Woodwork World' by the time I had left. It was *Charlie and the Chocolate Factory*-themed, the real one with Gene Wilder: "Come with me, into a world of imagination."

My Pioneer stereo completed the effect on the top shelf.

Quotes around the room included:

"Treat others how you would expect to be treated yourself"

"Perseverance"

"Believe and succeed"

"Come in and know me better, man"

"Don't forget, you are my number one student!"

"Life is like a journey, who knows where it ends?"

"Life is full of meetings and partings, that is the way of it"

"If you listen, enjoy, feel safe and work hard, you will learn"

"Jesus loves you"

"Those with two tunics should share with those who have none"

Put your mark down on your area.

29 My philosophy

Mum told me, "If a child is happy, feels safe and listens, they will learn."

This is the only philosophy I work with, even with the adults I was to lecture in evening class. I believe it to be true: when I think about how I learn, it resonates. You can dress it up into kinetic, verbal or visual learning, but it all returns to the above. It is also lovely and simple, and simple things often work best, especially before they are clouded by some psychologist. No matter what seating plans, assessment for learning, progress tracking, methods of feedback, special education needs, and independent learning techniques are in place, if you are happy...

I also used to concentrate on the students who wanted to learn first. Once they were on-board, I would then turn my attention to the 'non-doers'. Most would come around, but I certainly did not waste my time on the very few that would not. Often, to a non-worker I would say, "If you don't want to be here, go home," which my head of department was not too pleased with. Only one student took the offer up, but he was not allowed out at reception, so had to return. Many walked out of lesson, but after a short walk to calm down, would always return, mostly with an apology. Another DT colleague would always email a message to staff if a student had walked out of lesson. I never did this: it draws attention to the fact and often I was not bothered if they did not come back! That short time out of lesson gave the student a few minutes to chill out and think.

Sometimes, though, situations did get to me. One such situation was a Year Eight PE cover lesson playing basketball. I had a disruptive group who failed to listen or follow instructions. A basketball received my Bergkamp volley and my language to the group became a little choice. The head of year reported to me the next day that one of the students had been offended and that I had called them a bunch of 'bastards'.

My reply to him: "No, I actually called them a bunch of wankers."

Not at all professional I know, but sometimes that is how teaching makes you feel.

30 Extra-curricular

These events are more important than the usual timetable. Sports fixtures, clubs, events, trips, sports days, swimming galas. Untold, unmeasurable learning goes on at these. All go into the ethos of the school, something which is never put into the league tables. Friendship, trust, loyalty, comradery, respect, knowledge.

These activities show you in a different light to the students. You can show your real character if you wish. Some teachers did not like to show their true side, but I had no issues with it. How I was in the lesson, around the school, was how I was normally. I treated the students in my care no differently to how I treated my own children. In fact, whilst they were in my care, they were my children.

I remember spending my first sports day at Carlton Boys litter-picking all day. Cleaning up, so that when we left, we would leave a good reputation. Not always possible and not always done, but leading by example.

Swimming galas were great. An old tutee of one of my groups and now a PE teacher organised some great ones. The sixth-form students would help with the life-saving and some of us staff would also swim and save. It was fantastic to see the younger year groups look up to their peers setting a good example. Unmeasurable learning. Knowing my tutee from a Year Eight student, it was also great to see what he was achieving.

Many of my previous students have done well and often I am greeted with Mr C or Clarky when out and about in the local area. Not that I can remember them all, but it is always lovely to see and hear about them.

Darts club was most likely my best legacy there. The students were interested; it helped with their maths, younger years mixed with older. The pinnacle was the annual darts championship with trophies for the winner and runner-up. Yes, competition with winners and losers but always humble when winning and honest in defeat.

Get involved with the school outside of your usual environment. You will also learn new things.

31 Inset

"Bloody teachers, Inset days are a right pain. Why can't they do these days during holidays or weekends? I have to work weekends sometimes."

This quote was from my old foreman at Surrey Joinery when I was an apprentice in 1983. He was annoyed because he had to arrange childcare for his daughter during Inset days. As Mum was a teacher, I explained.

Well, at weekends there are often sports fixtures, also marking, assessment, reports, schemes of work and parents' evenings. (Untold marking if you are a primary teacher.) There are also school trips, residential with twenty-four-hour care. All of that overtime the teachers put in, after work, during weekends and holidays, they do not get any extra money for. You get paid for your overtime.

The foreman thought about it, looked at me and declared, "Ok, fair point."

Inset days were actually five days taken from the teachers' holidays, usually to complete some pointless activities. The students still get those days as holiday, but just spread over the year. As a parent I can appreciate that it was a pain. My children sometimes had to come to work with me.

Those early Inset days were pointless. Meet and discuss subjects that did not need discussion. As a DT department we could have used that time to prepare, sort, organise. That would have been far more useful. But did schools trust professional teachers to manage their own workload? Not in my early days.

At Carlton Boys, SMT did change the routine for Inset to a better format. It took some tweaking along the way, but Inset took place after school as evening sessions, allowing those five days to be put back with the holidays throughout the year. Those sessions were run by teachers who had theories to put across and explain, supposedly to improve you and ultimately the school. It was all part of your career planning, target-setting, points to discuss with your line manager. The way forward for you, and how the school could support your career development. My best planning, thoughts, were always when I was in 'my office'.

One such scheme was named 'Best to Better'. A teacher, taking the lead with four or five others discussing predetermined questions. The aim in the long run was to make you an outstanding teacher. On one occasion a lovely English teacher was our group leader. Our questions involved comparing how the geese flock and fly together to learning in education. I had fun that session!

It was all about progression to outstanding. As I always argued, is no one happy with just being good? I know I was. Students thought I was a good teacher and that was acceptable for me. Why be satisfactory some lessons, outstanding in others? The law of averages equates that to a level of good anyway. Why not just be good all of the time? That is the problem, constantly wanting you to improve, it gets tiring and you can feel underappreciated just being a good teacher. To be outstanding 100% of the time, mentally and physically, would kill you.

So Inset would be aimed at improving you as a teacher and ultimately also pushing your students to achieve their best which naturally, as a teacher, you would do anyway.

One assembly, SMT proudly announced that during a learning walk, a Year Nine maths group were doing Maths that they had not completed until their degree course. Well, I thought to myself, there is the problem with education. Too much, too soon.

On one of my last interviews to become a construction teacher, the school wanted the students to complete a level 2 qualification in carpentry and joinery. The same qualification a sixteen-year-old would take two years at college to achieve. Bearing in mind that the majority of those students had just struggled to mark out and cut a simple corner halving joint. The school was living in cloud-cuckoo-land. Too much, too soon.

Inset, suck it in and see: unfortunately it has to be done.

32 Jesus

When my dad passed away from cancer in 2008, Mr C looked after me well. Good people always think of others. As a child I had attended some sessions of Sunday school, but I was never a regular churchgoer. Lin, my better half, has more knowledge of the Bible from her mornings at Sunday school whilst her parents were in church. Lin still has a better knowledge of the Bible than me, even now.

In the summer of 2009, my eldest son Stephen and I embarked on a charity bike ride across America to raise funds for Cancer Research UK. For a time, we stayed with my Uncle J who is a devout Christian, heavily into the Lord. That time with him made me view life differently. Uncle J still took some views from the Old Testament, so my understanding of the Bible differs slightly. The Old Testament predicted what was coming and the New Testament superseded this with the views of Jesus (as I understood it anyway).

Did it affect my teaching and personality? I hope so. I did not think I was too bad a person but not perfect by any stretch. Finding Jesus, the Holy Spirit, made me less judgemental, more forgiving. (Forgiving, I will always struggle with that.) At school other colleagues had the Holy Spirit in a total way. I thank them for their love, support, encouragement and faith. The Holy Spirit is out there: hold out your hands and accept it.

That is not to say that if you are not religious you are a bad person, far from it. My other Uncle P is more scientist than religious, and is still a really great person, willing to help anyone at anytime with anything.

Going to church also does not make you a good person. Finding the selflessness from the Bible, looking after all others before yourself, not changing the words of the Bible to suit your own needs makes you a good person. It certainly is not easy. Accept Jesus and you, too, can be forgiven, but you will need to think of how you view life and what things are important. Some of the most hypocritical people are regular churchgoers. One day they may see the light.

So, digressing, is there life after death? At funerals people would say the deceased is looking down from above, watching your back in Heaven after entering the pearly gates. Believe me, that would be wonderful when both Lin and I have gone, meeting up there for eternity. That being the case, whilst living, this must be our Heaven. The last thirty-one years and hopefully many more with Lin are my Heaven.

I believe it is more a good spirit, the Holy Spirit. When we pass, stating the obvious, we are no longer here in body. I do not think we look down from the clouds: it is better than that. Our spirit is with the family, friends and loved ones we have been in contact with during our time in Heaven. We live on in their hearts. It is certainly difficult when someone you love is not here in body anymore. Not a day goes past when I do not miss Dad, but I often talk to him, especially when working. I know he is laughing at my attempts to repoint a window frame or skim a wall with plaster. Other family, friends and pets that I have known and lost are always with me.

When I go, I want my children, family and friends to continue living, enjoy good things, be nice people, think of others, look after each other. I will still be in their hearts. That will be the best way to honour me. Sadly, all living things die. I just hope that when my time comes, I am old, tired and ready for it.

As a teacher, you will also stay with many. The students' lives you affected for the better. We can always recall our best teachers. What better legacy to have?

Woodwork

33 Further education

Before I finally gave up on education, an opportunity arose at a further education college in Surrey. The position for a carpentry and joinery lecturer was vacant. In my interview, I was pipped at the post by another candidate. Only by a 'fag' paper, according to the head of learning at the time. That was in March. In June, the college contacted me. The joinery tutor was leaving so did I want the job? Bench joiner by trade, I accepted and took up the post in September.

College was a strange affair to start with, especially after working in a school environment. I was expecting it to be more relaxed, which it was to start with. The salary was not the same as teaching, but I knew that also. The big difference: as the tutor, you had to deal with a lot of the administration. Issues in school that would be dealt with by the good old office team. Register problems, admin info; organisation changed on a yearly basis, nothing seemed to remain constant. It was probably due to the office redundancies each year. It also was not long before Ofsted would rear its ugly head and the college started to become school-like in its requests, all to gain a better rating. The problem being, however, that the college was a huge beast across three sites and many subjects. Even if your part is top-notch, it proves insignificant if other areas of the college are not. Ofsted, 'K2' pinch of salt time!

The most significant problem with college was English and Maths. The college would literally get beaten up by Ofsted if students were not gaining English and Maths to the equivalent of pass grades. So some students who had just spent the last eleven years at school, with the full support of teaching staff and who had failed to obtain the right grade would have to resit the subjects and retake their exams along with their craft subject. If they did not pass, it affected the college figures. These figures again clouding the real work that went on inside. Students had come to learn a trade, get away from the school routine and be treated more like an adult. Failing English and Maths again demotivated many. In terms of trades, the college had a top team of tradesmen and women passing on their skills. I saw this first-hand and I know that any craft student was lucky to be there with the dedication of those teams.

Of course English and Maths are important in construction, but naturally some are brighter and more gifted than others. It is a natural order: some are stronger, some are more intellectual, and some are more practical. Education never seems to accept this fact, instead arguing that everyone can be good at everything, or should be. Even when your best fails to meet the grade, you must still get better. Trade work does not work like that. With trade work, there is a right way or a wrong way, nothing in-between. Do it wrong and you should fail, simple. So those students who struggled with English and Maths, but who were good with their hands, may make decent craftspeople and learn the appropriate skills and knowledge to survive in what they do. Those who did have English and Maths would do this also, but these students were also your supervisors and management in the making. It is a natural order.

I was also surprised in my first year by the group of bench joiners who signed up for the level 2 full-time course. Surprised because most of them did not want to be there and were still very immature. A group size of twelve, aged between seventeen and twenty-one. Only three of them had any real ambitions to become a joiner. The rest were there because they just had to be. Despite varying the theory lessons with different aspects and tasks, little aroused their interests. I was always on my guard during practical and machining sessions. They were working with machines that could easily prove fatal if they stepped out of line. The layout of the workshop and machine shop meant that when I was on my own, it was impossible to supervise both areas. Two of the better students became my eyes and ears and I gave them more time and input.

The apprentice group was better behaved that first year, but many were lazy and it was a battle to push them through. There was one exceptional student amongst the apprentices, a magical joiner with top-quality work for such a young age, naturally talented.

At the end of the first year, two of the full-time students failed as they had dropped out of the course. All of the others managed to pass. One student even took the time to write me a letter of thanks for helping him get through the course. (Poorly written as he had not passed his English!) He described me as a 'top bloke', so it was pleasing to know I had made a difference for one of them.

In the third year, I had eight students in the level 2 bench group. The college was struggling financially, so the construction block had been sold and joinery was moved into a shed closer to a new, smaller machine shop. Those eight students were the best group I had the privilege to teach. All had passed their English and Maths, all wanted to be there, all wanted to work and listen. I told them regularly, "You are my best group ever."

All passed the course and we did some brilliant extension work in the form of stairs, windows and cupboards. Some real-life work. From that group, three students returned to do the level 3 bench joinery. They completed this and more. If I need any help in the future with any work, I would have no problem working with any of those gents. All are top-quality.

As a bench joiner and tradesman, I also have a teaching degree. Further education establishments, though, need to accept that if they want tradespeople to come and share their skills, they will need to operate differently to schools.

Tradespeople should not have the burden of, 'Why is that student not going to pass? How can you get them to pass?'

It is the students' responsibility to learn from that tradesperson. If a student acts inappropriately and fails to work, they should be shown the door, regardless of the time of year, just as in the real world.

At the Surrey college, the first six weeks were the time supposed to weed out any bad students. After this time, due to finance and figures, it was not said out loud, but there was little chance of removing them. There may have been a written final warning or timed exclusion after this time, but rarely a full exclusion. During those first six weeks of the year, unhappy students were encouraged to 'swap, not drop'.

To attract good tradespeople into further education, the salary must be improved. You lecture students, passing on your skills and knowledge. These students can then go away and earn more money than you. How can that be right? Trade lectures deserve a salary of at least 45k.

Other than the time of day, 6 to 9 in the evening twice a week, the adult classes were always enjoyable. Why? They wanted to be there and they had paid to be there, so all wanted to listen and work. Many I took further with their own extension tasks. It was also a privilege to pass on the skills I had learnt to them.

34 Plenary

Every outstanding lesson has a starter, middle and a plenary, so we are led to believe. Within that time students/learners may well display red symbols or objects for 'I have not got a clue what I am doing'; yellow for 'I think I know'; or green for 'Yes, I understand completely'.

Practical time differs from the wanted lesson structure, however. Starter: blazers off, aprons on and come around the front bench, horseshoe-style so that everyone can see. Another DT colleague always had 'shrimps' at the front, 'lankiest' at the back.

Middle: practical work. Anyone not understand? Shout out (not literally) and I would help if a peer could not. By observation you could tell if a student was struggling, no colours required. Anyway, if a mistake was made, have another go. We always learn by making mistakes.

Plenary: work away, tools away, benches swept, blazers on. Stand by your benches and a few tool questions if we have time.

Before the word 'plenary' was ever mentioned, my early years at Carlton Boys involved many a Mars bar end-of-lesson question with my better Year Seven group. After clearing away and sitting down ready to go, I would give out a question. The prize for the first student to answer correctly was a Mars bar.

"Fun size, sir?"

"No, full size!"

The question would not be an easy one for that age group. In fact, they would have no idea. As a Gooner, it would also be about Arsenal and not recent Arsenal. Some examples:

Who scored the winning goal in the 1979 FA Cup Final?

What make of boots was Liam Brady wearing in the 1979 Cup Final?

Who got the winning goal against Juventus to win the Cup Winners' Cup semi-final in 1980?

It was a time before Google was on their phones and with no idea, it was always a mad scramble to find a PE staff member, or another Arsenal-supporting member of staff to see if they could give the answer. They would scurry back, not always with the right answer, to try and claim the prize. When Carlton Boys introduced healthy eating, the Mars bar plenary disappeared, and the carrot question did not have quite the same appeal!

The point I am trying to make is that as a teacher, develop your own style and routine that works for you. If you tried to implement every new initiative requested, you would go nuts. By all means try some, but only use what works for you. Some teachers as a form of control would like the students sitting down according to a seating plan and take the register at the start of the lesson. Once I knew the group, I would mark off as we went on during the lesson. As projects progressed, especially with the older years, often it would be a case of come in, work out and get on. Simple.

Some teachers would give detentions for no pen or pencil. I would not, there would be spares to use. Do not make life hard for yourself, being a teacher is hard enough. Have some fun with the students and have fun at their expense. Many a time in the DT department if a student was being a pain, we would send them to another DT colleague asking for:

"A long wait"; "The striped paint"; "The 100mm air hooks."

Some never caught on. I am not sure what the record wait time was.

So, if you are going to teach:
- Be yourself
- Be honest
- Be caring
- Do not be too serious
- Do not think your subject is the most important thing in the world
- Work to live, do not live to work
- Give yourself a cut-off time from work. What does not get done today can be done tomorrow

- Acknowledge your colleagues, all of them
- Remember that you were young once
- Remember that you hated some lessons at school, too!
- Do not take too much to heart or personally
- Enjoy your holidays
- Keep your payslips

My traditional views and values are no longer suited to secondary school teaching. I enjoy being valued for my practical skills as a good 'chippy'. At present I am due to start lecturing at a different further education establishment, but also continue with my carpentry and joinery work to further boost my salary!

As a final footnote, if you join the Teachers' Pension Scheme (TPS), check that they have a record that you are a member, have opted in and are aware of your salary. In 2006, TPS were made aware that I had opted back in since 2002. In 2018, when I checked to see what my pension is worth, they had no record of it, only that I had opted out in 1993 when I first started teaching. I had kept every single one of my teaching payslips since 2002. I could prove that I had paid over £41,000 into the scheme. This proof then had to go to my previous employers so that they could inform TPS of my opted-in status. Hassle, but thank you to James. Thank you also to my editor, Ben.

So you want
to TEACH?

First published 2019

Published under licence by Brown Dog Books and
The Self-Publishing Partnership, 7 Green Park Station, Bath BA1 1JB

www.selfpublishingpartnership.co.uk

ISBN printed book: 978-1-83952-072-3

Cover design by Andrew Prescott
Internal design by Andrew Easton

Printed and bound in the UK

This book is printed on FSC certified paper